SEPARATION

Benefits

of

Building Our Community

By Rasheed L. Muhammad

Co-Author Abdul Wahid Muhammad

Forward By Dr. Ridgeley M. Muhammad

Copyright©2018Rasheed/Wahid

7/12/2018

Contents

Why a book like this?

To understand the value of controlling our own community is the way to our future survival, public safety (*the welfare and protection of the general public expressed as our governmental responsibility*). Our prosperity and peaceful co-existence with one another must be re-enforced. A book like this provides more than enough insight to justify the benefits of building our own community.

What is a community?

Building a community is not an individual effort. A community is a small or large social unit of people who have something in common, such as norms, religious values & good practices. Such practices regarding *not what we say, but how we live to demonstrate* our life values or social identity.

Communities also share a sense of place that is situated in a given geographical area or in virtual space through communication platforms. Long lasting relations that extend beyond immediate genealogical ties also define a sense of community. Although communities are usually small relative to personal social ties, "community" may also refer to large group affiliations, such as national communities, international communities, and virtual communities.[1]

How to use this book

This book is a prerequisite to our seminar presentation. Sample slides have been included toward the

---

[1] https://en.wikipedia.org/wiki/Community

end of this book to aid you about how we shall conduct our seminars designed to make [us] and our offspring realize what a community looks likes and how to take control *(the power to influence or direct people's behavior or the course of events)* of our own community for wellness.

PART 1

Why Build Our Own Community

Building a community is based on plans prepared by qualified men and women. However, the greatest resource of a community are developed God given talents in every person of that community. By nurturing talents, the ultimate service and growth of a community's well-being equal unlimited progress for every man, women and child.

Rendering Community Plan Map

Building and controlling our own community relieves us from police brutality, mob attacks, financial exploitation by banks, poor schools, out dated education curriculum, drug dens, youth-murder, prostitution, pimping and others forms of social degradation. By building and controlling our own community, we can experience luxury, money, good homes and friendships in all walks of life, good manners and courtesy *(the showing of politeness in one's attitude and behavior toward others)*.

Later on in this book, we will discuss how we have the privilege to build our communities using ministries to govern therein after the pattern of God's creational pattern. As Minister Farrakhan said:

> *"After He [God] created Himself, then came our universe. So the pattern of the universe is after the pattern of [God] Himself. So if you want to study government, study how God made you…The solution is to model the government after the human body…created in Gods image.*

> *"If we study this magnificent body … we can relate all these 10 systems to 10 ministries with subgroups and tasks forces that will allow us the privilege of building our own communities."*[2]

Death Of The Ghetto By Gentrification

Many black and brown people are experiencing "GENTRIFICATION." Gentrification means displacement for lower-income families due to the rise in property values and rental costs. Displacement begins as landlords take advantage of rising market values and evict long-time residents in order to rent or sell to the more affluent.[3] In other words. Developers and bankers work hand in hand

---

[2] Holy Day of Atonement Lecture, 2009
[3] https://en.wikipedia.org/wiki/Gentrification

with city officials in the name of urban renewal. If one can afford the price to pay higher rates, urban renewal is great.

Before Gentrification

After Gentrification

Questions to think about!

1. How does a community fall into low-income status?
2. What are the social, cultural, educational, religious and economic practices of low-income residence?
3. What are the social, cultural, educational, religious and economic practices of those whom gentrify low-income communities?

Black People Once Built Communities Separating From White Oppression

Appendix 1, on page 78, remarks the reason why the first Black Town in the United State of America was established. Read it before going forward!

PART 2

Blacks Have Built Own Communities

President Abraham Lincoln emancipated (*The act by which one who was unfree. or under the power and control of another, is set at liberty and madeliis--be ones own master--.* America's slave population in the year 1865. Subsequently, from 1865 to 1877 and beyond, knowledgeable (*intelligent and well informed*) black men and women built 200 towns under their own power and control after being emancipated to escape slavery, suffering and death at the hands of white authority. Post-civil war black communities were not segregated from white communities, they separating from white communities to assure the benefits of unity in our community that is **Harmony, Integrity, & Industry.**

By 1888, at least 200 black towns and communities had been established nationwide. Some were modeled on black towns that had been formed after the American Revolution and during the antebellum era — from the late 1700s to 1860.

"The black-town idea reached its peak in the fifty years after the Civil War," Norman L. Crockett wrote in his book "<u>The Black Towns</u>."

One of the most renowned Black communities was Greenwood, Oklahoma (Black Wall Street). It generated a variety of thriving businesses such as **600 businesses,**

grocery stores, clothing stores, barbershops, banks, hotels, cafes, 1 hospital, 6 private airplanes, movie theaters, two newspapers, its own school system and many **contemporary homes.** Greenwood residents enjoyed many luxuries that their white neighbors did not, including **indoor plumbing** and a **remarkable school system.** The **dollar circulated 36 to 100 times,** sometimes taking a year for currency to leave the community.[4]

Black Communities Established Post-Civil War

Rosewood, Florida (1923)

Rosewood was a quiet, self-sufficient whistle-stop on the Seaboard Air Line Railway in Florida. Blacks had three churches, a school, a large Masonic Hall, turpentine mill, a sugarcane mill, a baseball team and a general store (a second one was white owned). The village had about two dozen plank two-story homes, some other small houses.

Washington, D.C. (1919)

Washington's Black community was then the largest and most prosperous in the country, with a small but impressive upper class of teachers, ministers, lawyers and businessmen concentrated in the LeDroit Park neighborhood near Howard University.

Knoxville, Tennessee (1919)

An African-American business district.

New York City (1863)

Owned homes and businesses and had a growing political, economic and social power.

---

[4] https://blackthen.com/8-successful-and-triving-black-communities-destroyed-by-racist-white-neighbors/

Durham North Carolina (1800s and early 1900s)

They built Lincoln Hospital, staffed by black doctors and nurses, as well as a theater, a library, hotels and over 200 businesses.[5] North Carolina Central University was founded in Haiti in 1910 and became the first liberal arts HBCU to be state-funded in 1925. Black Wall Street was a four block district on Parrish Street nicknamed in reference to the district of New York City. Although the term "Black Wall Street" did not become prevalent until the late fifties, its identity as an economic powerhouse for blacks was apparent since the late 1800s. Numerous other cities in the south had similar black economic centers, including Tulsa. Parrish Street bordered the Haiti community, Durham's main African American residential region. The two areas together served as the center of black life in Durham.[6]

Birmingham, Alabama (1950's)

Downtown area of Fourth Avenue, known as the Black Business District. The area, also known as "Little Harlem," boasted retail shops, attorneys, doctor's offices, a half-dozen hotels and much more. The buildings were designed by black architects and built by black construction companies, including the six-story structure built by the black-owned Penny Savings Bank.[7]

At the center of the black community was the Church, it was the moral compass for family structure and the local economic and educational system. Black women upheld the does and don't regarding how to act at home and abroad. It was a time when immoral acts were clarified and

---

[5] https://www.theroot.com/the-other-black-wall-streets-1823010812

[6] https://en.wikipedia.org/wiki/Black_Wall_Street_(Durham,_North_Carolina)

[7] https://www.theroot.com/[object%20Object]

at least carried out in private, away from the general public and children.

> ## U.S. Systematic Destruction
> ## Of Black Community
>
> After 1877, the unprecedented progress of Reconstruction by many Black Communities was attacked physically and then legally destroy by jealous whites. These whites were subsequently backed by local government authorities and paid money.

The "Compromise" of 1877

Rutherford B. Hayes is given the Presidency when Republicans agree to:

1. Name a Southerner to Cabinet

2. Federal spending on rebuilding South

3. Remove military from the South

The removal of troops = the end of Reconstruction!!!

U.S. law maker's legal war against Black Communities after 1877 led to the infamous Jim Crow laws, which were state and local laws in the United States enacted between 1876 and 1965. Jim Crow laws existed mainly in the South and originated from the **Black Codes** that were passed from 1865 to 1866 and from prewar segregation on railroad cars in northern cities.[8] The U.S. Government and Banks decided on February 26, 1877 to give/lend money to former southern slave owners (including Jewish slave owners[9]). The money was to cover losses for their freed slaves. In addition, U.S. federal troops, placed in the south to protect newly released slaves, were removed — relieved of duty. Consequently, Southern Black Codes became LAW and the Emancipation Proclamation counted for nothing. RECONSTRUCTION ENDED!

southern Black (odes

Directions: With a partner, read the following examples of black codes that were used in southern states to restrict the rights of freed slaves. Answer the discussion questions.

1. Prohibited marriages between whites and freedmen.
2. Segregation in public facilities, cemeteries, schools, and any form of transportation.
3. Racial segregation in public cemeteries.
4. Freedmen over the age of 18 were required to have a job or could be fined and put in prison.
5. Freedmen could not assemble together without the presence of a white person.
6. Illegal to teach freedmen to read or write
7. Freedmen could not own guns or any other forms of weapons.
8. Freedmen couldn't obtain certain jobs (shopkeeper, artisan, mechanic) unless they paid for a license.
9. Prohibited from voting.
10. Prohibited from owning property

---

[8] https://en.wikipedia.org/wiki/Black_Codes_(United_States)
[9] Secret Relationship Between Blacks and Jews Vol. 1 & 2

Questions to think about!

1. **Why did white citizens of America and their local government authorities destroy post-civil war black communities after 1865?**

Jim Crow (Black Code) was actually more potent than the Civil Rights Legislation Act of 1964 and the Voting Rights Legislation Act of 1965. Of the two Acts, a third Act was never mentioned or missing. The missing Act was the return of the land taken from Blacks because of Jim Crow laws which ended the Reconstruction. Land up to amounts of 16 million acres before U.S. government backed white predators were state sanctioned to retake the land.

Protect, Respect And Elevate The Black Woman

Photo Courtesy of Black Atlantic Star Newspaper

Imagine what these black women were thinking when the Black man was "gentrified" (removed) off his land and property. Imagine what the black man was thinking as he walked away helplessly from white land predators. Moreover, what were the white land predators thinking? Naturally, they were thinking how they'd develop the land taken from beneath the foot of the black man and his woman.

<u>The question is:</u> Why was LAND not returned to the Black Communities as a third part of the Legislation Acts? And, how has integration ruined the black community?

Black Wall Street before Destruction, 1921

Black Wall Street after Destruction, 1921

Questions to think about!

1. What is the difference between segregation and separation?
2. How have black women and girls been treated?
3. How must the black women be protected?

PART 3

Maintaining Community Is Warfare

Historically and currently, the United States Governmental policies and actions evince that a plan and plot to ruin black communities is warfare. Let us begin, for time sake, such acts of warfare began in 1738 to current in spite of negotiations by leaders of the black community.

Warfare comes in many ways. For instance, with inner-city expressways, the destruction of low-income housing began. This plot originated in the Bureau of Public Roads (BPR), the federal agency established in 1919. Thomas H. MacDonald, a highway engineer from Iowa, headed the BPR from its founding until early 1953.[10]

---

[10] https://flh.fhwa.dot.gov/about/history/car/

Historically speaking, take Miami, Florida's, state highway planners and local officials whom deliberately routed Interstate-95 directly through the inner-city black community of Overtown. An alternative route utilizing an abandoned railroad corridor was rejected, as the highway planners noted, to provide "ample room for the future expansion of the central business district in a westerly direction," a goal of the local business elite since the 1930s. Even before the expressway was built, and in the absence of any relocation planning, some in Miami's white and black press asked: "What about the Negroes Uprooted by Expressway?" The question remained unanswered, and when the downtown leg of the expressway was completed in the mid-1960s, it tore through the center of Overtown, wiping out massive amounts of housing as well as Overtown's main business district, the commercial and cultural heart of black Miami.[11]

Other black communities that also fell victim under the Bureau of Public Roads (BPR) were as follows:

1) *North Nashville black community*, destroying hundreds of homes and businesses and dividing what was left of the neighborhood

2) North Claiborne Avenue in central New Orleans, an old and *stable black Creole community*, boasting a long stretch of magnificent old oak trees, North Claiborne served a variety of community functions Poverty & Race Research Action Council Civil Rights Research 2002 22 such as picnics, festivals, and parades. The highway builders

---

[11] http://www.prrac.org/pdf/mohl.pdf

rammed an elevated expressway through the neighborhood before anyone could organize or protest.

3) Interstate construction in *Montgomery, Alabama, also devastated a black community.* In 1961, state highway officials recommended a route for Interstate-85 that traversed the city's major African American community. George W. Curry, a black minister and head of a Property Owners Committee, sent a petition with 1,150 signatures to local, state, and federal highway officials protesting that the expressway route would destroy an estimated 300 homes in black Montgomery and proposing an alternative route through mostly vacant land.

4) The expressway story was much the same in Columbia, South Carolina. In 1968, the *South Carolina NAACP organized the Columbia black community* in protest over the route of the Bull Street Expressway, an Interstate-20 link that penetrated the central city. Franchot Brown, a black community leader in Columbia, charged the South Carolina Highway Department with "a general pattern of racial discrimination" in attempting "to restrict the Negroes to the ghettos."

5) A similar pattern of planned destruction took place in *Camden, New Jersey,* bisected in the 1960s by Interstate-95, with the usual consequences for low-income neighborhoods. In 1968, the Department of Housing and Urban

Development sent a task force to Camden to study the impact of highway building and urban renewal. It found that minorities made up 85 percent of the families displaced by the North-South Freeway — some 1,093 families of a total of 1,289 displaced families. For the five year period 1963 to 1967, about 3,000 low-income housing units were destroyed in Camden, but only about 100 new low-income housing units were built during that period.

The above report was released by *The Interstates and the Cities: Highways, Housing, and the Freeway Revolt* by Raymond A. Mohl. The Department of History, University of Alabama at Birmingham further records numerous other black communities destroyed in the name of urban renewal in the following cities:

- Kansas City, Missouri, Model City area
- Charlotte, North Carolina, African American community
- St. Paul, Minnesota, Interstate-94 cut directly through the city's black community
- Los Angeles, California, dislocate 3,550 families, 117 businesses, and numerous parks, schools, and churches, mainly in black Watts and Willowbrook
- Pasadena, California displaced over 4,000 black and Mexican-American resident
- Tampa, St. Petersburg, Jacksonville, Orlando, and Pensacola Florida divided, and dislocated black

- communities, or permanently walled them off from white neighborhoods
- Columbus, Ohio, an inner-city expressway leveled an entire black community.
- Milwaukee, the North-South Expressway cleared a path through sixteen blocks in the city's black community
- Cleveland, Ohio
- Chicago, Illinois
- Atlanta, Georgia
- Washington, D.C.
- Baltimore, Maryland
- Philadelphia, Pennsylvania

In short, the U.S. Government appropriated black people's tax dollars to ruin black communities across America! I reiterate, in spite of the public and legal protest made by black community leaders opposing "Expressways via their communities," they were denied a victory. While at the same time, many white community leaders, whose protest against expressways through their communities, prevailed.

Questions to think about!

1. **How many billions of dollars did the U.S. Government borrow from the Federal Reserve Bank to destroy Black Communities in the name of Expressways?**

PART 4

Post-Civil War
Black Professionals &
Educators

Brave men and women have come and gone since slavery in America. There have been untold leading men and women during slavery and after slavery. All yearned to see Blacks controlling their own communities and businesses in their own territory i.e., self-governance. Some we cannot name, others we can name. For instance:

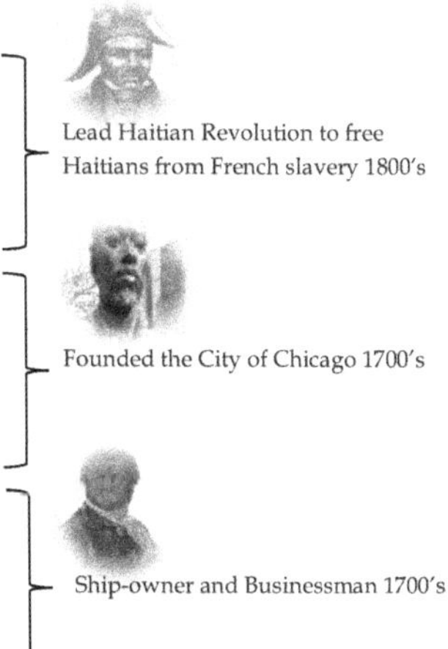

1. Toussaaint L' Ouverture
2. Jacques Dessalines
3. Henri Christophe

Lead Haitian Revolution to free Haitians from French slavery 1800's

4. Jean B. P. De Sable

Founded the City of Chicago 1700's

5. Paul Cuffe

Ship-owner and Businessman 1700's

6. Denmark Vesey
7. Nate Turner
8. William Still
9. Harriet Tubman
10. Sojourner Truth

Led U.S. Southern slave Revolt 1700's and bravery journeys to land areas of liberty

None of these men and women were cowards or quislings

Fredrick Douglass - Alexander Crummell - Roberts Smalls – Hiram Revels – Robert B. Elliot – Elijah McCoy – Grantville T. Woods – Madame C. Walker – Maggie L. Walker – A. G. Gaston – Ida B. Wells – Marcus A. Garvey

If you can tell yourself who George Washington is but not recognize five of the names and contributions of the brave men and women mentioned above, you might be a victim of amnesia, spiritual lepers, white lies and fairly tells.

Questions to think about!

1. Who was George Washington fighting against and what was he fighting for?
2. Who were post-civil war black leaders fighting against and what were they fighting for...separation or integration?

Other ethnic groups build their own communities. This means their fighting to maintain dominance over their own business districts?

Maps of Ethnic Towns in Modern America

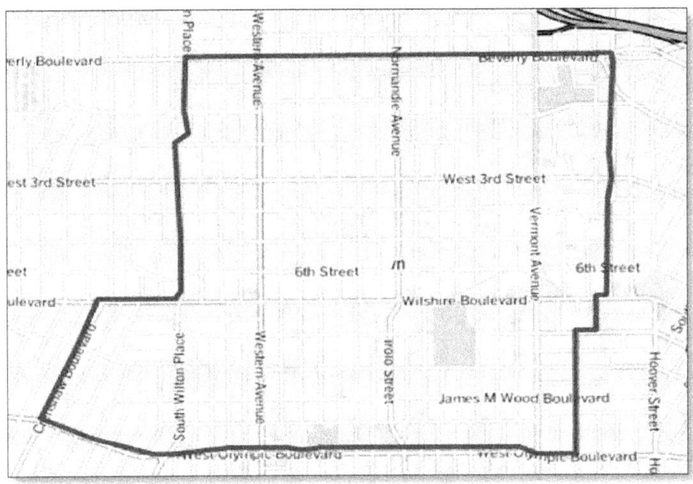

Korea Town Territory of Los Angeles, California est. 1980's

Little Armenia Los Angeles, California est. 1970's

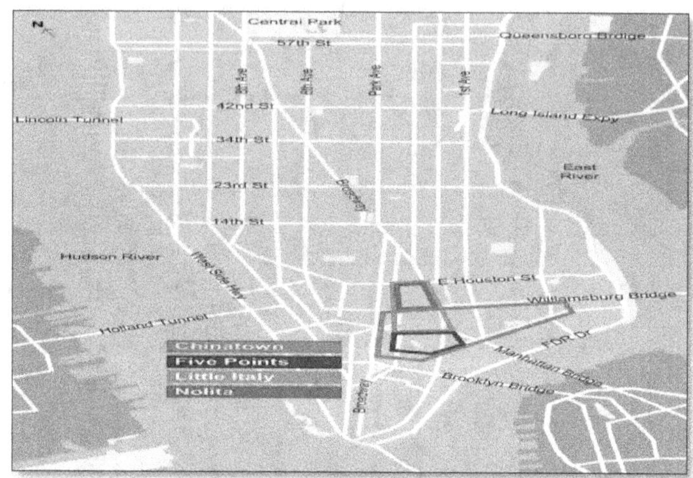

China Town, Little Italy New York, New York est. late 1800's

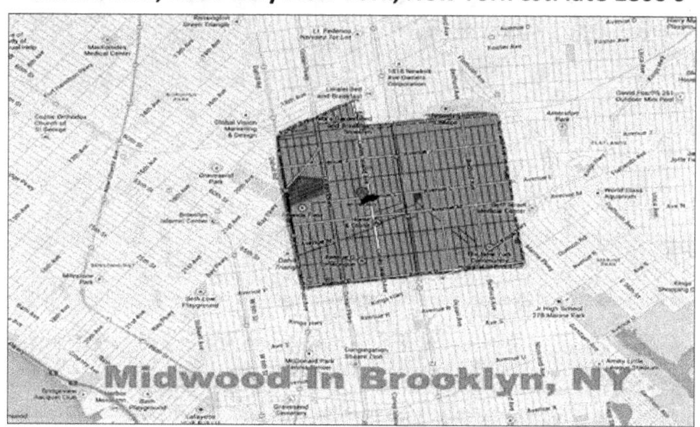

Jews of Midwood, Brooklyn, NY est. 1990's

A little note about the East Midwood Jewish Center, a Conservative synagogue, was founded in 1924. The building, located on Ocean Avenue, is a 1929 Renaissance revival structure with a capacity of 950 in the main sanctuary. It was listed on the National Register of Historic

Places in 2006.[15][16] The Kingsway Jewish Center is an historic synagogue from the 1950s on Nostrand Avenue. It was listed on the National Register of Historic Places in 2010.[12]

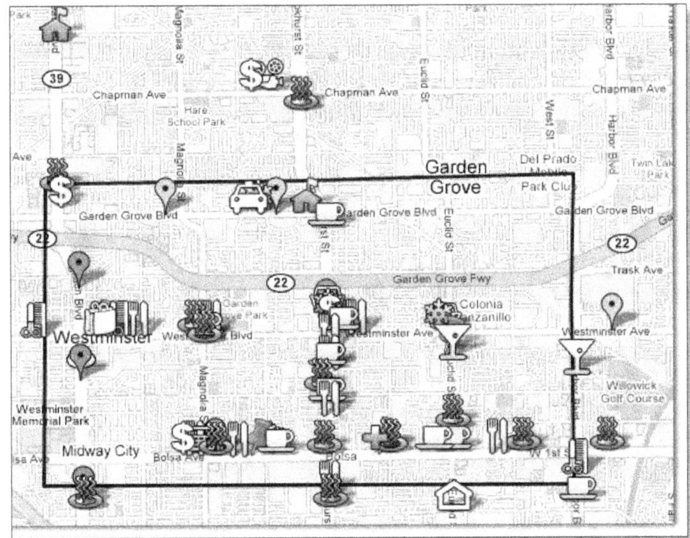

Little Saigon est. in USA 1980's

A special note about Little Saigon; which is the most well-established and largest Vietnamese-American enclaves, must also be highlighted. Their business districts not all of which are called Little Saigon, are in Orange County, California; San Jose, California; and Houston, Texas.

Somewhat-smaller communities also exist, including the comparatively nascent Vietnamese commercial districts in San Francisco, San

____

[12] https://en.wikipedia.org/wiki/Midwood,_Brooklyn#History

Diego, Atlanta, Sacramento, Denver, Oklahoma City, New Orleans, the Dallas–Fort Worth metroplex (Haltom City, Arlington, and Garland), Falls Church, Virginia, Orlando, and Seattle.[13]

High crime rates and wanton violence reduces a communities options to attract consumer traffic to patronize its business operations and overall economic health.

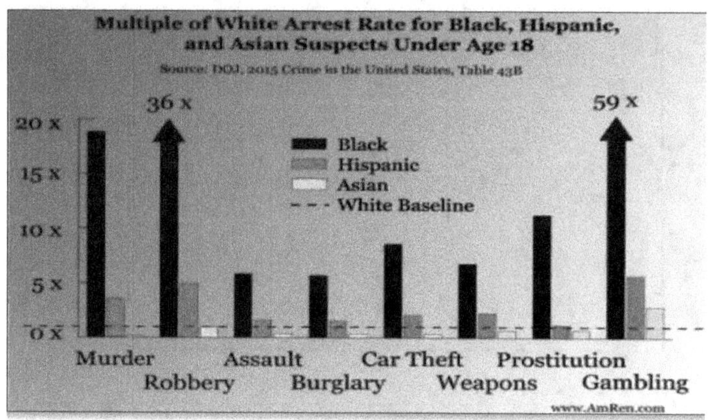

When one visits said ethnic self-controlled territories or business districts of Jews, Chinese and others, you'll find operating beneath their community infrastructure are several basic systems i.e.

SPIRITUAL DEVELOPMENT
(according to their own nature]
Agriculture
Education
Information

Health
Trade and Commerce
Defense
Justice
Arts and Culture
Science and Technology

---

[13] https://en.wikipedia.org/wiki/Little_Saigon

These systems are active for (1) community growth, (2) development and (3) self-empowerment. Are there crimes being committed in said communities? Yes. Nevertheless, said ethnic groups believe *(to accept something as true, genuine, or real)* in a nation within a nation infrastructure that is rooted in their cultural collective consciousness. Therefore crime does not override their survival tactics for community economic stability. Are their base areas of economic operations isolated? No. Do they allow all members of society to spend money with them? Yes. Have their community business operations become multi-million dollar profit centers? Yes. Do they desire to see you in their communities? Maybe, maybe not.

Questions to think about!

1. Provide location of 3 Black economically controlled business districts in North America where people spend money?
2. What are the statistical crime rates of said ethnic communities compared to that of the "black" community?
3. Are U.S. towns such and China town, Little Italy, Korea Town and the like established based upon common descent, history, culture, racism or militant talk?

PART 5

Nation of Islam In North America

At age 34, Elijah was taught by Master Wallace Fard Muhammad, the Great Mahdi of the Muslim world and Messiah of the Christian, over a 3.5 year period of time from 1931 – 1934. This process occurred in Detroit, Michigan. He taught Mr. Elijah Muhammad that black people were literally fulfilling the  final portion of divine scripture and that the white race were a race of devils whom had captured and destroyed black people. This was mentioned in both Bible and Holy Quran. Moreover, he taught the 5'6" 120 lbs. Elijah how to establish and maintain the foundation called the Lost and Found Nation of Islam of Islam in North America.

 After U.S. authorities realized whose presence Master Wallace Fard Muhammad (W.D. Fard) represented and fulfilled, he was arrested in Detroit, Michigan, in 1933, for "**Conversion.**" You ask why? White authority

felt they still owned black men, women, boys and girls as personal property. They were upset because the Son of Man had arrived amongst the lost and founds.

What is CONVERSION?

Answer: This term applies to taking another person's property without any cause or permission. It is an unlawful action.[14]

By 1934, Master Fard Muhammad departed without a trace. However, Elijah Muhammad was prepared as His servant, to oversee the Lost and Found Nation of Islam in North America that is independent of devils, out of the Europe, religious (cosmological) interpretation.

Elijah Muhammad Arrested In 1942

Years later, the FBI initiated a search for Master Fard Muhammad (W.D. Fard) to no avail. In 1942 they decided to arrest the Hon. Elijah Muhammad in Washington D.C. on May 8th. In his oral statement to special agents Muhammad mentioned that W.D. Fard instructed his followers not to register for Selective Service. The Bureau's Washington Field Office then contacted Detroit and suggested checking the Detroit Police Department records for a criminal record, photographs, or any information they might have on Fard and his whereabouts.

The Detroit Field Office checked the records of the Identification Division of the DPD and discovered that a Wallace Fard was arrested in Detroit for "conversion" on May 26, 1933. His serial number there was 45138. He was

---

[14] The Law Dictionary

described as "White Male, 33, 127 lbs, 5'6", Slim build, black hair, maroon eyes, Arabian." W.D. Fard was thus recognized by the DPD as a white skinned *Arab*.

On May 16, 1942 the Detroit office raided NOI Temple #1 located at 623 Medbury Street; agents confiscated a picture of the Flag of Islam and of Master Fard Muhammad. These would help, the Bureau hoped, to "positively identify Fard." On September 20, 1942 the FBI raided the Hon. Elijah Muhammad's Chicago home and confiscated two more images of Fard. These photos along with the mug shot from the Detroit arrest made available to the FBI on August 8, 1942 were displayed to individuals in hopes of making identifications and of locating Fard.[15]

Photo of Elijah Muhamad handcuffed and arrested, 1942

After nearly five years, Elijah Muhammad was released from Federal Prison in 1946 and began rebuilding the community and economic foundation of the Nation of Islam. Chicago, Illinois is where he began along with its registered members and friends alike. During the 40's and

---

15

http://www.finalcall.com/artman/publish/Perspectives_1/article_6699.shtml

50's, in Chicago, Illinois, a bakery was established on 31st and Wentworth St., Temple No. 2 on 43rd street, Temple No. 2 Grocery store and restaurant on 71st street. Also Muhammad University of Islam School was established.

Photos Courtesy of Accomplishments of The Muslim Magazine

> ## Final Call To Islam Newspaper Cost 3¢ 1934
>
> This Newspaper was published weekly by Elijah Muhammad, Minister of Islam in North America. Its Editor, John Ali, Manager, Wali Mohammed, Writing Staff, Sis. Burnsteen Sharrieff, Kallatt Mohammed, Lonnie Pasha.
>
> Office Address: 283 E. Hancock Ave, Detroit, Mich.

As you can realize, the nascent internal business structure of the Nation of Islam assured that its Headquarters would be financed to upkeep all vital governmental provisions. Its business operations were established within the black community open for patrons.

Questions to think about!

1. Was the Nation of Islam in North America established by former sharecroppers and descendants of former slaves?
2. Why did the U.S. Government arrest Master Fard Muhammad and the Honorable Elijah Muhammad?
3. Was/Is the Nation of Islam's economic program a threat to the United States Government?

PART 6

Nationhood Leadership

The Honorable Elijah Muhammad was led by his teacher, Master Fard Muhammad, to announce the land that the Muslims want. In the following statement, he published:

1. We want freedom. We want a full and complete freedom.
2. We want justice. Equal justice under the law. We want justice applied equally to all, regardless of creed or class or color.
3. We want equality of opportunity. We want equal membership in society with the best in civilized society.
4. We want our people in America whose parents or grandparents were descendants from slaves, to be allowed to establish a separate state or territory of their own–either on this continent or elsewhere. We believe that our former slave masters are obligated to provide such land and that the area must be fertile and minerally rich. We believe that our former slave masters are obligated to maintain and supply our needs in this separate territory for the next 20 to 25 years–until we are able to produce and supply our own needs.

Since we cannot get along with them in peace and equality, after giving them 400 years of our sweat and blood and receiving in return some of the worst treatment human beings have ever experienced, we believe our contributions to this land and the suffering forced upon us by white America, justifies our demand for complete separation in a state or territory of our own.[16]

Questions to think about!

1. What is a full and complete freedom?
2. Since 1865, did black people receive equal justice under white authority?
3. What is equal membership in society?
4. What is a civilized society?
5. How does "what the Muslims want" amplify the main Act never mentioned in the Civil Rights Acts of 1964-65?

15 Million Acres Of Land Swindled Away

In Pete Daniel's book titled *"Dispossession: Discrimination Against African American Farmers in the Age of Civil Rights."* He writes, Africans were released into the bowels of a wretchedly racist society after having been enslaved for centuries in the United States. Four [400 years] decades later, after organizing around the strategic need of land possession to build a better future for themselves and future generations, they managed to accrue some 15 million acres of land, mostly in the southeastern region of the country.

Land ownership by those Africans living in the United States, according to The Nation, served as farms, the primary occupation for most in the early 20th century. By

---

[16] https://www.noi.org/muslim-program/

1920, 14 percent of all farms in the country, representing approximately 925,000 farms, were owned by Black people.

However, the impressive number of Black farmers and rural landowners would drastically decrease over the 20th century. During that century, so often touted as being a groundbreaking Black civil rights movement, some 600,000 Black farmers were forced off their lands. The Nation reported that by 1975, only 45,000 Black-owned farmers remained.

Jim Crow, Black Codes and other forms of institutional and societal racism also factored into arbitrary seizure of land owned by Black people due to their lack of access to legal measures and the courts to properly obtain a title to the land.

Nation Of Islam For Black America

Moving progressively out of the 1930's, 40's, 50's 60's and into the mid 1970's, the Honorable Elijah Muhammad, a few progressive professionals, a few educators, a few celebrities, a few revolutionaries and thousands of registered members of the Nation of Islam manifested a blueprint for all black America to reduplicate.

In fact, the chart on the next page exemplifies the accomplishments of the Nation of Islam from 1965 to 1975 by investing the nickels, dimes and dollars donated to Mr. Muhammad to invest. We will delve further into Mr. Muhammad's Economic Blueprint in Part 8 of this book.

***No government grants nor loans were procured by the Nation of Islam to build such a foundation of a nation within a nation infrastructure for Black America's benefit.**

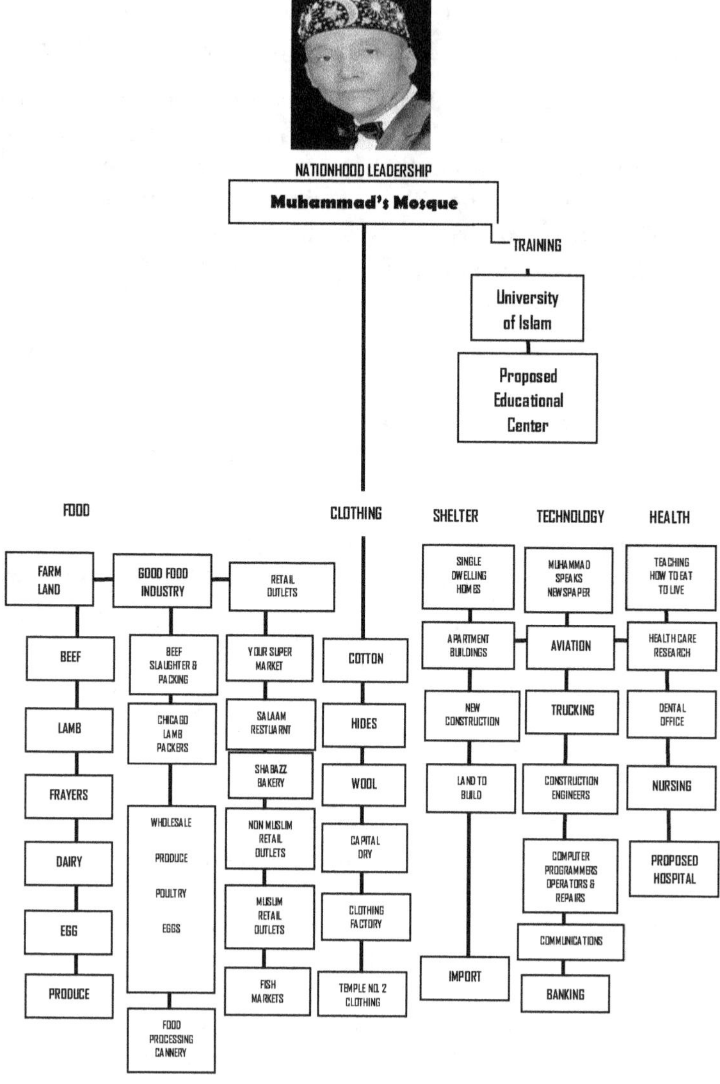

NATIONHOOD LEADERSHIP
Muhammad's Mosque
TRAINING
University of Islam
Proposed Educational Center
FOOD
CLOTHING
SHELTER
TECHNOLOGY
HEALTH
FARM LAND
GOOD FOOD INDUSTRY
RETAIL OUTLETS
BEEF
BEEF SLAUGHTER & PACKING
YOUR SUPER MARKET
COTTON
SINGLE DWELLING HOMES
MUHAMMAD SPEAKS NEWSPAPER
TEACHING HOW TO EAT TO LIVE
LAMB
CHICAGO LAMB PACKERS
SALAAM RESTUARNT
HIDES
APARTMENT BUILDINGS
AVIATION
HEALTH CARE RESEARCH
FRAYERS
SHABAZZ BAKERY
WOOL
NEW CONSTRUCTION
TRUCKING
DENTAL OFFICE
DAIRY
WHOLESALE PRODUCE POULTRY EGGS
NON MUSLIM RETAIL OUTLETS
CAPITAL DRY
LAND TO BUILD
CONSTRUCTION ENGINEERS
NURSING
EGG
MUSUM RETAIL OUTLETS
CLOTHING FACTORY
COMPUTER PROGRAMMERS OPERATORS & REPAIRS
PROPOSED HOSPITAL
PRODUCE
FOOD PROCESSING CANNERY
FISH MARKETS
TEMPLE NO. 2 CLOTHING
IMPORT
COMMUNICATIONS
BANKING

Reviewing the Nationhood Leadership Chart above, take note how it represents an infrastructure of a nation within a nation concept as other ethnic communities have demonstrated. Furthermore, no government loans or grants were procured to achieve those ends. Moreover, you might notice the 10 basic systems for community growth, jobs, self-development at work as well:

1) Spirit Development (Center of activity)
2) Agriculture
3) Education
4) Information
5) Health
6) Trade and Commerce
7) Defense
8) Justice
9) Arts and Culture
10) Science &Technology

At the center of these Nation of Islam community blueprint of accomplishments is Mosque activity and then training. Nothing new here because the Church was once at the center of past black community accomplishments during the early post-civil war era. Hence, the need for this book, *"Benefits of Building Our Community From Death To Life."*

Questions to think about!

1. Who raised and backed Honorable Elijah Muhammad to lift his community?
2. Why is the Mosque or Church or Temple to be at the center of community activity?
3. What type of training is necessary to build a community?
4. What spiritual education did Mr. Muhammad use to build the men and women of the Nation of Islam?

Accomplishments and Plans By Nation of Islam

Photos Courtesy of Accomplishments of the Muslim Magazine

Through education, our community will lead in medicine, technology, geometry, mathematics, chemistry, physics, urbanization, art, poetry and moral culture. Moral the principles of right and wrong behavior of human character) being the operative word.

Elijah Muhammad's Greatest Preacher

Economic development combined with moral and spiritual education propelled the NOI to show signs of progress with the establishment of farms, livestock and vegetable cultivation, rental housing, private home construction and acquisitions, other real estate purchases, food processing centers, restaurants, clothing factories, banking, business league formations, import and export businesses, aviation, health care, administrative offices, shipping on both land, sea and air, and men's and women's development and leadership training units. By 1972, the Nation of Islam had a net worth of $75 million plus dollars. At today's rate of inflation, in 2018, makes that *$356,248,554.91*.

Young Minister Louis X was placed over Muhammad's Temple No. 7, New York City at age 32. He was named National Representative of the Honorable Elijah

Muhammad in 1965 after the Government of the United States assassinate Minister Malcolm, not to mention the role carried out by Gene Roberts, the self-admitted government agent provocateur and Malcolm X body-guard.

> *"...A 1992 CBS news special featuring Dan Rather interviewing those who've interacted with the late, great Malcolm. X. In the video, Dan speaks with Gene Roberts, who was an undercover police officer, ordered by his superiors to try to get as close to Malcolm as he possibly could.*

> *Roberts got very close to Malcolm, actually becoming his bodyguard by taking advantage of his trust. In the video below, you can hear Robert's explain why he and other government officials were worried that Malcolm might incite violence, and why they were working so hard to track his every movement. The most interesting part of the discussion stars at the 13:45 mark in the video, but the rest of it is fascinating as well.*[17]

---

[17] http://yourblackworld.net/2015/05/04/malcolm-xs-former-bodyguard-was-also-a-government-informant/

With no uncertain terms, Gene Roberts admits he was one of Malcolm's chiefs of security, as well as a NYPD undercover cop on the day Minister Malcolm was assassinated.

The chaos that ensued two days after Malcolm X was murdered led to the destruction of Muhammad's Temple No. 7. It was firebombed and destroyed.[18]

Fortunately a sectarian war between Muslims who loved Malcolm and Muslims who loved The Most Honorable Elijah Muhammad did not ensue, as the perpetrators had envisioned...After the destruction of Temple No.7 The Most Honorable Elijah Muhammad assigned Minister Louis X (later named Farrakhan) to New York in 1965 to rebuild the Muslim community and the Temple (Mosque) building itself, which was reopened in 1969.

Questions to think about!

1. **Why did the black community of Harlem, New York avoid fighting and killing one another after Malcolm X was murdered?**
2. **Why did Gene Roberts suggest to Malcolm X not to search people coming into the Audubon Ball Room[19]?**
3. **By age 42, what form of talent did Minister Farrakhan demonstrate to signify he was**

---

[18] NOI held meetings on 106 West 127th Street.

[19] In the basement of the Audubon Ballroom was also a synagogue called Emez Wozedek and was there from 1939 to 1983. http://hhoc.org/audubon-ballroom/

born to lead and rebuild broken communities, people and alliances?

At age 32, Minister Farrakhan was tried by fire. His rebuilding efforts in New York included one of the more than 20 Muhammad University of Islam schools established by the Muslims in the 5 boroughs of New York. Temple No. 7, at street level the building included a restaurant, bakery, and convenience store. You could find Steak n Take restaurants and Shabazz Bakeries all over New York. Under Minister Farrakhan's leadership Temple No. 7 imported millions of pounds of whiting fish from Peru and "fed the multitudes" in New York. The number of Muslim followers of The Most Honorable *(worthy of honor and high respect; estimable; creditable)* Elijah Muhammad grew far beyond the levels accomplished while Malcolm X was the New York minister.[20] All Minister Farrakhan's accomplishments were under Muhammad Mosque leadership?

Minister Farrakhan Speaks To 70,000 People May 27, 1974

The occasion was "Black Family Day" on Randall' Island, New York. New York City Officials were so frighten they thought the Muslims were going to capture New York City.

Little did Minister Louis Farrakhan know that his innate capability to re-establish New York's Nation of Islam

---

[20] http://noirg.org/articles/how-the-bombing-of-temple-no-7-relates-to-the-911-false-flag-operation/

community and black people in general and love to work with organizers prepared him for his next major assignment? His next major assignment would be to rebuild the Nation of Islam after its destruction by the U.S. GOVERNMENT et alia (and the others) in 1975.

Yes, the Nation of Islam was destroyed by U.S. Governments counter-intelligence "programmers" operating from within the heads of men and women holding positions of authority. But the Nation of Islam rose again by the great power of Allah!

PART 7

Death To Life
Rebuilding Community

After the destruction of the Nation of Islam's community business and original spiritual infrastructure, the counter-forces of darkness within the U.S. Government never expected to it re-established as other black communities have never been re-established to their former glory. Take for instance, Black Wall Street of Tulsa, Oklahoma, 1921 and others towns mentioned in Part 3 of this book. But to the surprise of many, the Nation of Islam has been re-established and recognized around the world by its friends and enemies.

After avoiding an assassination plot, the Honorable *(of high rank, dignity, or distinction; noble, illustrious, or distinguished)* Minister Louis Farrakhan Muhammad was touched by an angel in 1977. Thereafter, he began rebuilding the Lost and Found Nation of Islam according to the teachings of the Most Honorable Elijah Muhammad. The result has been a success in spite of the U.S. counter intelligence program and Zionist Jewish & most hateful Gentile opponents of the Nation of Islam and the Black community in general.

As it were, when Minister Farrakhan began rebuilding the community of what is called the Nation of Islam in 1977, he literally began with nothing. Of course, his experiences in Harlem New York, beginning in 1965, also prepared him mentally to uphold his mission. But only this time around, the second time around, there were no Temples, schools, businesses, FOI (men and women of Islam), National House, Headquarters, Secretary, Captains and Lieutenants. No Economic development, farms, livestock, rental housing, private home construction and business acquisitions. No real estate purchases, food processing centers, restaurants, clothing factories, banking, business league formations, import and export businesses, aviation, health care, administrative offices, shipping on both land, sea and air, and men's and women's development as his teacher, Elijah Muhammad had established from 1934 to 1975. The 75 million dollar national infrastructure of the Nation of Islam was no more; nothing!

I think it should be said at this point, I once recall having a conversation with Mr. Jim Brown[21], who said, the greatness of Minister Farrakhan is what he accomplished…i.e. "he brought the nation back from nothing." He admirably  recollected how he observed the Minister walking around his (Jim Brown) swimming pool playing the violin, contemplating and deciding to rebuild the Nation of Islam.

---

[21] Former NFL Champion, community advocate and business man.

Minister Farrakhan's Rebuilding Strategy and Achievements Since 1977

- Strengthened The Brotherhood of the Nation of Islam
- Founded Final Call Inc., Newspaper
- Recaptured Nation Headquarters and National Residence of Nation of Islam in Chicago, Illinois and Phoenix, Arizona
- Re-established Muhammad University of Islam schools
- Introduced POWER Concept
- Purchased Farm Land in Michigan and Georgia
- Traveled World Making Friends for Black America
- Re-established Mosque and 120 study groups around the U.S. Europe, Caribbean, and missions in West Africa and South Africa
- Held a gathering of nearly 2 million men in Washington DC
- Declared Black People the Real Children of Israel
- Exposed the modern day Synagogue of Satan
- Released a 44 song album "Lets Change The World"

N.O.I. Representative's 1 Billion Dollars Blocked

In 1996, the United States Government legally banned the Honorable Minister Farrakhan from receiving 1 Billion Dollars from Africa's Libyan Government.

"Clinton Administration officials said today that they would almost certainly reject an application from the Nation of Islam and its leader, Louis Farrakhan, to be allowed to accept a donation of more than $1 billion from Col. Muammar el-Qaddafi of Libya.

"Mr. Farrakhan defended the gift today and said he would mount a vigorous fight if the Government barred it.

'"We will fight for what we believe is our legal right,'' Mr. Farrakhan told a news conference in Chicago, ''and I will go across the nation stirring up not only my own people, but all those who would benefit from it.''

''We are not terrorists,'' Mr. Farrakhan said. ''We are not trying to do anything against the good of America. What we want to do is good for our people and ultimately good for our nation.''

"A number of people affiliated with the Nation of Islam said they believed they would have a strong case that a rejection would be an unconstitutional infringement on religious freedom.

"Colonel Qaddafi pledged $1 billion to the Nation of Islam after meeting with Mr. Farrakhan in Libya in January. Mr. Farrakhan has described the pledge as a ''humanitarian'' gesture, and last week he formally asked the Office of Foreign Assets Control at the Treasury Department for the necessary permission to receive the money. The United

States, which has long labeled the Qaddafi Government a supporter of terrorism, bars nearly all economic ties with Libya.

"After his news conference today, Mr. Farrakhan left on a return visit to Libya, where he is scheduled to receive an award from Colonel Qaddafi. Officials said Mr. Farrakhan's application to the Treasury Department includes a provision to receive the $250,000 honorarium the Libyan award carries in addition to Colonel Qaddafi's $1 billion pledge.

'''Considering who we're dealing with here, a betting man would not be wise to bet on license approval,'' said one Government official familiar with the application. ''He would bet the ranch on litigation thereafter.'''

Questions to think about!

1. Why did the United States Government authorities block Colonel Qaddafi's 1 Billion Dollars earmarked for the Nation of Islam and its National Representative, Minister Farrakhan?
2. Why Colonel Qaddafi was ultimately murdered U.S. backed rebels?
3. Why has the media published the Nation of Islam National Representative, Minister Farrakhan net worth at 3 million dollars?
4. In what manner does Minister Farrakhan carry a nation on his shoulders?

Net Worth Of U.S. National Representatives

For those whom admire their U.S. Representatives for looking out for the welfare of our communities, I have provided a list of their 2015 net worth to say "thanks for everything you do" for the black community.

This ***list of members of the United States Congress by wealth*** includes only the fifty richest current members of Congress and displays the difference between assets and liabilities for the member and his or her immediate family, such as a spouse or dependent children. These figures can never be entirely accurate, because the financial disclosure requirements for the United States Congress are approximate by design. The original documents for each member's disclosure are publicly available on a database website, maintained by the Center for Responsive Politics. In 2015, to rank among the top 50 wealthiest members of Congress required a net worth of at least $7.28 million.

Source: Roll Call (2015)[1]

Rank	Name	Party	State	Net Worth ($ million)
1	Rep. Greg Gianforte	Republican	Montana	315
2	Rep. Darrell Issa	Republican	California	254.65

Source: <u>Roll Call</u> (2015)[1]

Rank	Name	Party	State	Net Worth ($ million)
3	Rep. Michael McCaul	Republican	Texas	107.61
4	Rep. John Delaney	Democratic	Maryland	91.68
5	Sen. Mark Warner	Democratic	Virginia	90.85
6	Rep. Jared Polis	Democratic	Colorado	90.81
7	Rep. David Trott	Republican	Michigan	73.52
8	Sen. Richard Blumenthal	Democratic	Connecticut	66.99

Source: <u>Roll Call</u> (2015)[1]

Rank	Name	Party	State	Net Worth ($ million)
9	Sen. <u>Dianne Feinstein</u>	<u>Democratic</u>	<u>California</u>	52.78
10	Rep. <u>Vern Buchanan</u>	<u>Republican</u>	<u>Florida</u>	49.86
11	Rep. <u>Diane Black</u>	<u>Republican</u>	<u>Tennessee</u>	45.95
12	Rep. <u>Scott Peters</u>	<u>Democratic</u>	<u>California</u>	40.19
13	Rep. <u>Alan Grayson</u>	<u>Democratic</u>	<u>Florida</u>	33.86
14	Rep. <u>James Renacci</u>	<u>Republican</u>	<u>Ohio</u>	31.62

Source: <u>Roll Call</u> (2015)[1]

Rank	Name	Party	State	Net Worth ($ million)
15	Rep. <u>Suzan</u> DelBene	<u>Democratic</u>	<u>Washington</u>	31.02
16	Rep. <u>Nancy</u> Pelosi	<u>Democratic</u>	<u>California</u>	29.35
17	Rep. <u>Roger</u> Williams	<u>Republican</u>	<u>Texas</u>	27.45
18	Rep. <u>Tom</u> MacArthur	<u>Republican</u>	<u>New Jersey</u>	25.90
19	Rep. <u>Rodney</u> Frelinghuysen	<u>Republican</u>	<u>New Jersey</u>	24.73
20	Rep. <u>Chris</u> Collins	<u>Republican</u>	<u>New York</u>	23.83

Rank	Name	Party	State	Net Worth ($ million)
21	Sen. Jim Risch	Republican	Idaho	19.14
22	Sen. Claire McCaskill	Democratic	Missouri	19.10
23	Rep. Joseph Kennedy III	Democratic	Massachusetts	18.64
24	Sen. Bob Corker	Republican	Tennessee	17.98
25	Sen. John Hoeven	Republican	North Dakota	17.54
26	Sen. Ron Johnson	Republican	Wisconsin	17.00

Source: <u>Roll Call</u> (2015)[1]

Rank	Name	Party	State	Net Worth ($ million)
27	Sen. David Perdue	Republican	Georgia	16.78
28	Rep. Richard Hanna	Republican	New York	16.13
29	Rep. Don Beyer	Democratic	Virginia	16.01
30	Sen. John McCain	Republican	Arizona	14.41
31	Rep. Fred Upton	Republican	Michigan	14.32
32	Rep. Kenny Marchant	Republican	Texas	13.91

Source: <u>Roll Call</u> (2015)[1]

Rank	Name	Party	State	Net Worth ($ million)
33	Rep. Jim Sensenbrenner	Republican	Wisconsin	13.52
34	Rep. Lloyd Doggett	Democratic	Texas	12.94
35	Rep. Nita M. Lowey	Democratic	New York	12.03
36	Rep. Scott Rigell	Republican	Virginia	11.40
37	Rep. Trent Franks	Republican	Arizona	9.85
38	Rep. John Fleming	Republican	Louisiana	9.64

Rank	Name	Party	State	Net Worth ($ million)
39	Sen. Johnny Isakson	Republican	Georgia	9.51
40	Sen. Mitch McConnell	Republican	Kentucky	9.41
41	Rep. Curt Clawson	Republican	Florida	9.30
42	Rep. Carolyn B. Maloney	Democratic	New York	9.15
43	Rep. Mike Kelly	Republican	Pennsylvania	8.73
44	Rep. Bill Foster	Democratic	Illinois	8.32

Source: <u>Roll Call</u> (2015)[1]

Rank	Name	Party	State	Net Worth ($ million)
45	Sen. <u>Ron Wyden</u>	<u>Democratic</u>	<u>Oregon</u>	8.24
46	Sen. <u>Rob Portman</u>	<u>Republican</u>	<u>Ohio</u>	8.05
47	Rep. <u>Buddy Carter</u>	<u>Republican</u>	<u>Georgia</u>	7.87
48	Rep. <u>Rod Blum</u>	<u>Republican</u>	<u>Iowa</u>	7.86
49	Rep. <u>Tom Rooney</u>	<u>Republican</u>	<u>Florida</u>	7.76
50	Rep. <u>Steve Pearce</u>	<u>Republican</u>	<u>New Mexico</u>	7.73

Questions to think about!

1. What is the role of a U.S. representative to U.S. communities and how do they get paid or compensated?
2. How does the U.S. Government generate money?
3. Do United States Representatives have a right to access wealth for representing U.S. community needs?
4. Do United States Representatives family members have a right to work for their family businesses?

> ## Black Entertainers are also Representatives of their people. Many work hard to avoid this reality due to being apprehended.
>
> See Appendix 2, on page 80, Net worth of Black Celebrities, according urbanintellectuals.com

PART 8

Your Community Blueprint

The Honorable Elijah Muhammad said that the FARM in the engine to our national life [of a community].

How To Fund Muhammad's Economic Blueprint

Muhammad's Economic Blueprint as shown throughout this book, is what has enabled the Nation of Islam in North America to lay down a foundation as a nation within a nation. Their paradigm is for black America's own salvation and redemption to get from under white authority, disrespect and vulgar world. Living within own communities means security and a circle of divine safety. Mr. Muhammad's economic blueprint is designed to help black people help ourselves in the battle to create jobs and end poverty and want.

Under Presidents Donald's Trumps America, it is clear what Black America must do for ourselves. We must think in similar terms to our post-civil war black leaders, professionals and educators and realize integration into the white man's social construct is not going to work out for us. Integration is has been against the **Harmony, Integrity and Industry** gained by Black America's post-civil war and pre-civil rights era promising communities.

Under Muhammad's wise economic plan and spiritual training, one is compelled think black, love black and be black. Simply do the math black! With 5¢ a day, 35¢ a week, $1.40 a month and $18.20 a year multiplied by 16 million wage earners would give us $291,000,000 in one year! Everyone can give 35¢ a week as an investment in their future. [22] There is no elaborate corporate scam or hidden fees to fund our own community development.

How Is U.S. Government Funded

How is the United State Government partly funded? By appropriating, on averages, 0.28 cents to 0.38 cents per wage earner to run its government, including paying government representatives and employees. According to **Office of Management and Budget**, the U.S. governments will collect **$3.422 trillion** for fiscal year 2019.

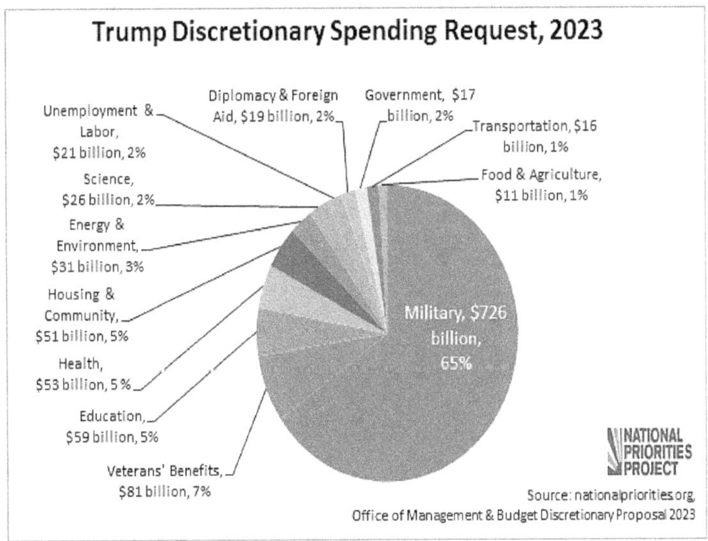

---

[22] http://www.economicblueprint.org/

How will some of the U.S.'s 3.422 trillion tax dollars aid in rebuilding black communities? **Answer:** *Since slavery began, no U.S. funding has helped to sustain the well-being of black communities.*

Do For Self

The challenge is start building where we have been segregated since integration, express freeway plots and redlining post-civil rights. Our success will be determined by each community's harmony, integrity, industry, talents, professionals, and educators, revolutionary thinkers and honorable spiritual leaders working in unison. No baby Bible or Quranic babbler nor philological debaters will solve our communities' inner conflicts. Cooperation and self-determination gives all 47 million plus black people the best opportunity. State by state, the Black Community must organize to build their own communities as other ethnic groups now boast. They make no public display of disunity on YouTube or Facebook on disagreeable matters or religious interpretation over and above their community ties.

The map on the following page illustrates where black people predominately live; namely, the southern states. Again, Mr. Muhammad's historical works in the south is bar none. His Economic Blueprint can yield success when applied rightly. Take for instance, Nation of Islam Pioneer, Minister Abdul Rahman Muhammad, the "ROCK of the SOUTH." He has the wherewithal concerning how to make fearless men and women build a safe environment for black people to reside.

"Min. Abdul Rahman Muhammad was raised in segregated Atlanta, GA in the 1930s and 40s, and joined the Army in 1950 during the Korean War.

"After returning to the U.S., in 1955 he heard and accepted the teachings of the Hon. Elijah Muhammad in Atlanta, and traveled to cities such as NYC, Detroit, Los Angeles before moving to NOI headquarters in Chicago in 1958.

"He rose up the ranks of the FOI from private soldier, lieutenant, first officer to captain and was a part of "the Honor Guard" of Temple #2 responsible for the security of the Hon. Elijah Muhammad as the Messenger traveled the country.

"The Messenger made Rahman National Investigator of all the Temples, and a buyer for NOI Farms in the South, where he took residence in Miami in 1961 and met and became a mentor and trainer of Muhammad Ali and brought him into the Nation of Islam, and also developed a close friendship with Min. Malcolm X and Min. Louis Farrakhan.

"In 1969 Hon. Elijah Muhammad made Rahman the Minister of Atlanta, GA, responsible for reforming the Black Man in the South and building the empire of the Nation of Islam in the Southern Region. Where he brought a new Temple, new School, had thousands of Muslims and established Muslim businesses all throughout the South.

In "1981, Min. Abdul Rahman joined the Hon. Min. Louis Farrakhan to help successfully rebuild the Nation of Islam and the teachings of the Hon. Elijah Muhammad, and he *remains steadfast as a Teacher and Reformer of His People."*[23]

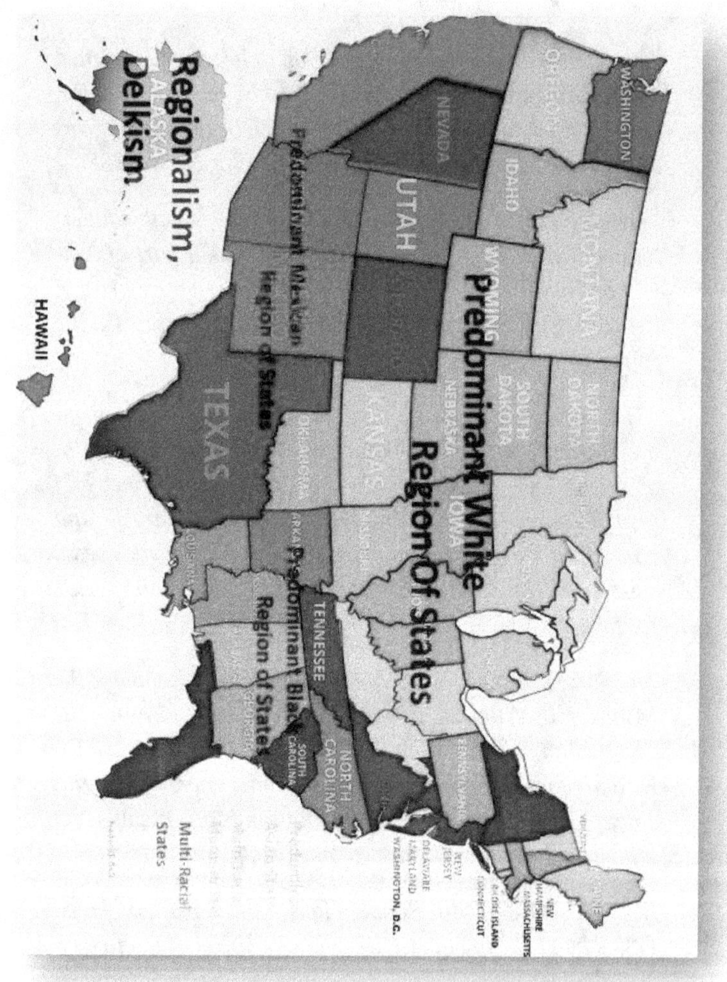

---

[23] http://www.blogtalkradio.com/allahteam/2015/12/18/foi-series-interview-w-min-abdul-rahman-muhammad-noi-pioneer-of-the-south-1

Separation Or Death

Black America is at a point of in its 450 plus year sojourn in North America wherein we must not segregate, but we must separate from under white authorities, folkways, morays and wrong-ways. Separate from her alcohol bottle, cigarettes, the strip clubs and perversion, the prostitution, the metro gender bender culture, the fake emotional hatred of one another, the white man's drugs and his pagan way of life[24], her phony religious and racial dialog without action to reform behavior problems.

Separate from the European holiday spending, swine and bad foods, the public verbal abuse, calling each nigga and bitches, vulgarity, public display of ignorance, child neglect, and constant consumerism with people who mean us no good. Separate from America's two party child-like juvenile delinquent political system and form our own community network that works for us!

Separate to agree upon and live with moral standards of a community rooted in values, beliefs, behaviors, experiences and expectations of good manners. In our own communities, we will live for life and not fall victim to so many untimely deaths by police justifiable homicide or senseless black on black crimes of passion or self-hatred to the delight of white supremacy. Their pattern, we have lived under since being brought to the America's is

---

[24] 1 Corinthians 12: [1]Now about the gifts of the Spirit, brothers and sisters, I do not want you to be uninformed. [2]You know that when you were pagans, somehow or other you were influenced and led astray to mute idols..."

Greek Democracy, Roman Ideas and Talmudic Jewish Law. It's no wonder we have been catching hell all these years. As a whole, black people have put into practice all we have learned and been taught under white authority.

Certainty, our contribution has helped to build this concrete material world we call America. So rather than verbalizing solutions for the Anglo Saxon[25] world order, how about putting forth efforts and knowhow to practice a new pattern as suggested by Mr. Muhammad's National Representative, the Honorable Minister Louis Farrakhan Muhammad, to build our own concrete material community! WE HAVE THE QUALIFIED MEN AND WOMEN TO DO SO!

Congressional Black Caucus

Invaluable brilliant minds to Black America's Future once he and she remove the rusty locks from around their own necks.

10 Ministries of The Nation of Islam

A *Ministry* is a collective executive. It is responsible for providing public service in a specialized field of government, led by a senior public servant known as "minister". The verb 'minister' is from a Latin word meaning "to serve". The noun 'minister' refers to one who provides a service as an agent of a higher authority. Ministries afford or give things needed by the people to help sustain an acceptable quality of life in the

---

[25] The early Anglo-Saxon period includes the creation of an English nation

society they serve. They are the practical means through which every member of the society receives freedom, justice and equality in his or her daily life and their existence insures a cohesive, flourishing society that improves and advances, generation after generation, toward the ultimate goal of complete freedom, justice and equality for all persons, regardless of creed or class or color.[26]

In 2009, during the Holy Day of Atonement address in Memphis, Tennessee, the Honorable Minister Louis Farrakhan gave us a key to whose pattern to apply when building our own communities. He said, in part:

"After He [God] created Himself, then came our universe. So the pattern of the universe is after the pattern of [God] Himself. So if you want to study government, study how God made you…The solution is to model the government after the human body…created in Gods image.

"If we study this magnificent body … we can relate all these 10 systems to 10 ministries with subgroups and tasks forces that will allow us the privilege of building our own communities."

The Bible 1 Corinthians 27-31 says, *"Now you are the body of Christ, and each one of you is a part of it. [28] And God has placed in the church first of all apostles, second prophets, third teachers, then miracles, then gifts of healing, of helping, of guidance, and of different kinds of tongues. [29] Are all apostles? Are all prophets? Are all teachers? Do all work miracles? [30] Do all have gifts of healing? Do all speak in tongues? Do all interpret? [31] Now eagerly desire the greater gifts."* Of course, communities consist of more than just apostles, prophets, teachers,

---

[26] https://www.noi.org/the-ministries/

healers and language experts. Communities also need, doctors, engineers, financial experts, diplomats, mechanics, law enforcers, nurses, artists, bankers, aviators, farmers, truckers, business entrepreneurs, administrators, day-care workers, scientist, etc., etc. So where do we go from here?

The Ministries are as follows:

1.   SPIRITUAL DEVELOPMENT

This Ministry bears responsibility for assisting the individual member of the community in the process of heeding truth and right guidance. Respect, honor and obedience to the Authority of the Creator in all aspects of life are essential to peace, harmony, freedom, justice and equality. In the words of the Honorable Minister Louis Farrakhan: *"...Self-development is an absolutely essential component of this microcosm of the new world. It is not enough that we grow horizontally through the acquisition of farms, factories, banks, industry, trade, commerce, money, good homes...horizontal growth alone is death. All dead things are on a horizontal level. Therefore, we must grow vertically: grow in uprightness, or we will be overcome by our horizontal growth."* The foundation of this ministry are study and training units, *"...designed on the Guidance of Allah (God) to produce: self-examination; self-analysis; self-correction and to quicken in each of us, the self-accusing Spirit. For it is only when we are awakened morally that we have to face the self-accusing spirit that leads to our resurrection."* (see, Letter of Introduction : <u>*Self-Improvement: the Basis for Community Development*</u>, December 12, 1986.)

2.   Agriculture

The Ministry of Agriculture is responsible for the development and maintenance of a system of sustainable agriculture to provide wholesome, natural food to the members of society. In addition to food, this Ministry is responsible for the production of raw materials required to build good homes and manufacture clothing.

3.   Education

The Ministry of Education is responsible for the mental and moral development of the members of the society by means of formal instruction in a prescribed manner over a prescribed period of time in a system of learning ranging from pre-school through primary through advanced academic levels, culminating in the conferring of academic degrees, under the direction of a National Board of Education. In addition to academic instruction, students shall receive teaching and training in the way of righteous conduct, decency and self-respect, with the goal of making a better nation of people.

4.   Information

The Ministry of Information is the central agency which provides services that include the development of all sources for informing the public of the policies, plans and strategies necessary for the free flow and accessibility of information essential to an informed and empowered citizenry. This includes collection, research and dissemination of current events, history, analysis; the publication of books, pamphlets, magazines and use of the internet and social media. It is also responsible for the development of information systems and networks to secure internal and external communications, media program development and management and establishment of an office of media affairs and press secretary.

5.   Health

The Ministry of Health and Human Services provides for the physical, mental and emotional well-being of the members of the society. The goal of the Ministry of Health is the fulfillment of the intention of the Creator for every human being to achieve his or her potential for both longevity and good health throughout life. Its efforts extend to the family and the community as well as the individual.

6. *Trade and Commerce*

The Ministry of Trade and Commerce is responsible for the growth and development of the business and economic interests of the society. This ministry is dynamic in nature, relying on the input of consultants with experience and success in business and economics. It analyzes the economic state of the community and develops programs and policies for growth and stability on the basis of the needs of the community. It translates skills, talents and interests of the community into viable revenue streams and works with the Ministry of Education to encourage entrepreneurship.

7. *Defense*

The Ministry of Defense ensures the safety, security and survival of the society and its members and develops policies and systems relating to the national security of the society, beginning with insuring safe and decent local neighborhoods. It is also charged with enhancement and protection of military and intelligence assets, structures and institutions.

8. *Justice*

The Ministry of Justice protects the rights and privileges of the members of the society and provides for penalties to be imposed upon persons who violate or threaten to violate the law or disrupt the peace. No member of the community shall forfeit his or her rights and privileges of membership in the community without just cause and without due process in reaching a determination that such cause exists. This Ministry is charged with the development of an independent judicial system in order to carry out its charge. It also initiates legal action, including class actions, against external entities, including governments, corporations, institutions and/or individuals, who, through their actions, pose a threat to the essential rights of members of this community.

9. Arts and Culture

The Ministry of Arts and Culture is the promotion of aesthetic, artistic and cultural expression in way that facilitates mental, emotional and moral upliftment of the members of the society. It includes visual and performing arts, including, but not limited to, music, film, dance, drama, literature, poetry, visual arts and sports. It includes promotion of theater companies, audio/video recordings, presentations, competitions and compilations and an annual Festival of the Arts. It extends to a wholesome sports culture for athletic competition and achievement.

10. Science and Technology

The Ministry of Science and Technology is the continuous development of technological resources, i.e., the application of scientific knowledge to the solution of human problems.

This Ministry embraces the broad discipline of Engineering and its sub-disciplines, including civil engineering, the design and construction of public and private works, such as airports, roads, railways, water supply and treatment, bridges, dams and buildings. Also, chemical, electrical, aeronautical and mechanical engineering.

This Ministry will also utilize information technologies to improve overall efficiency of all ministries, including the use of web sites and webcasts. This division will work closely with the Ministry

Europeans Jews and Gentiles
Federal Reserve Banking System

Black people have been misused by the rulers of the white race that have used their own quasi-private banking system to finance their own world of dreams, hopes and heavenly resorts on earth while at the same time build expressway through black communities that have yet to economically recover.

of Information to develop standard IT protocols and operating procedures and encourage technological education and training.[27]

To get involved with building our own communities, it begins with knowing how and where to contribute to Muhammad's Economic Blueprint.

Questions to think about!

1. **How is the farm an engine to nationhood and community prosperity?**

Farming And Community Is Key To Endure

Dr. Ridgely Muhammad, Farm Manager and his wife, Sis. Ann provide their expertise to oversee the Nation of Islam farming operation.

"Our 1556 acre farm in Georgia must be viewed as the catalyst for the development of our sustainable food and fiber production system. Muhammad Farms is situated on a 1556 acre tract in Southwest Georgia redeemed by Minister Louis Farrakhan in 1995 for the Three Year Economic Program. It is part of a larger 4500 tract of land which the Honorable Elijah Muhammad purchased in the 1960's.

"Muhammad Farms stretches1.45 miles east to west and 2 miles from north to south. To get the size of the farm in perspective, the farm is as long as Central Park in New York

---

[27] https://www.noi.org/the-ministries/

City or the Mall in D.C. but three times as wide. It would cover 23 city blocks in one direction and 16 blocks in the other direction. Four college campuses the size of N.C. A&T in Greensboro, N.C. could comfortably fit into its perimeters. Its area would cover 1400 football fields...[28]

Imagine if you will that a community be developed around modern farms. What would it like? Could it be a community of refuge to allow people to enjoy away from the major cities? Is it possible? Who's heading this effort?

"According to the Urban Land Institute, about 200 agriculture-centered developments have been built or are under construction, the vast majority since 2000, when the farm-to-table movement started taking off. Agritopia, near Phoenix, is 15 years old and more than 1,300 residents strong. All have access to a CSA supplied by a 22-acre farm on the property, and anyone — resident

---

[28] http://noimoa.com/muhammad-farms/

or not — can rent a 400-square-foot community garden plot for $250 annually. Currently all 41 plots are leased."[29]

Questions to think about!

1. Why is everyone making progress, yet we seem to be lagging so far behind?
2. Would you donate a $1.40 per week to the Nation of Islam's Treasury to finance each of the Ten Ministries?

As hundreds of Muslims from around the country converged on the pristine, picturesque property of Muhammad's Farm for a comprehensive agricultural seminar, it was evident to the men and women who enrolled, that this would be no ordinary weekend. The excitement on the faces of both participants and farm staff was a reflection of the warmth and brightness of the sun that radiated throughout both days…

A participant shoveling woodchips for compost.

… You have started on a great journey, the Minister told participants. "This is what God, Allah wants us to do and if you go back to the Genesis…People

---

[29] https://modernfarmer.com/2015/08/planned-agricultural-communities/

talk down about farmers as a derogatory profession, Min. Farrakhan pointed out.

Today, Blacks are not a part of agricultural business in comparison to Whites explained Betsy Jean Farrakhan. "We're trying to change that dynamic because less than one percent of us are in the Ag business so Insha'Allah we're going to change that around," she said. "We're going to teach you how to grow, even out of a bucket so don't even worry. Whatever your situation is, no matter how small or large the principles pretty much are the same and you'll be able to use those techniques throughout."[30]

---

[30] http://www.finalcall.com/artman/publish/National_News_2/article_102507.shtml

Appendix 1

First Black Town in United State of America

Henry Louis Gates, Jr. | Originally posted on The Root an Article of fact that between March and November of 1738, Spanish settlers in Florida formed a town named Gracia Real de Santa Teresa de Mose, two miles to the north of St. Augustine. Initially, it consisted of 38 men, all fugitive slaves, "most of them married," who had fled to Florida for sanctuary and freedom from enslavement in the Carolinas and Georgia. It came to be known as Fort Mose...

...Fort Mose was manned entirely by armed black men, under the leadership of Francisco Menendez, who became the leader of the black militia there in 1726. It deserves to be remembered as the site of the first all-black town in what is now the United States, and as the headquarters of the first black armed soldiers commanded by a black officer, who actively engaged in military combat with English colonists from the Carolinas and Georgia.

Menendez was born a Mandinga in West Africa at the end of the 17th century. He was captured and served as a slave in South Carolina until the Yamasee Native Americans fought the British settlers in 1715, during which Menendez managed to escape to St. Augustine, Fla. In 1738, he became the leader of the free black town, and was formally commissioned as captain of the free black militia of St. Augustine.

... "As news of the foundation of Mose spread through the South Carolina plantations, groups of slaves broke loose and tried to make for Florida." And, indeed, in November 1738, 23 men, women and children escaped from Port Royal, S.C., to St. Augustine. Gov. Montiano refused to return them to their supposed "owners," just as his predecessors had done since 1687. In March 1739, four more slaves and an Irish servant also made their escape to St. Augustine using stolen horses.

Spanish Florida was the African-American slaves' first Promised Land...

...On Sunday, Sept. 9, 1739, about 20 slaves, hailing (historians think) from Angola, killed two store attendants and stole arms and ammunition at Stono Bridge, south of Charleston. As they marched south heading toward Florida, their ranks swelled to about 100, and they continued to burn plantations and kill white settlers. A ferocious battle with the colonial militia left a field of death, including 20 of the colonists and 40 of the slaves. Slaves who fled were later captured and beheaded. But not even this unfortunate outcome deterred other slaves in the region from seeking their freedom: In June 1740, about 150 slaves rebelled near the Ashley River, just outside of Charleston. Fifty were captured and hanged.

Outraged by actions of the slaves at Stono, and fearful of more rebellions from slaves seeking to escape to Florida, the English countered with a siege of Florida between 1739 and 1740. They captured Fort Mose in 1740. As Landers reports, Captain Menendez and the Fort Mose militia allied with Native Americans to fight the invaders, culminating in a bloody battle in June 1740, in which Menendez and his forces attacked the British and killed 75 of their men. In the process, Fort Mose was destroyed...

Appendix 2

Net Worth of Black Entertainers

The Black entertainer always come to realize that he or she is put into a type of custody once they crossover into a certain financial threshold and media status. To remain in the money, the protocol is *denial* particular social realities or be demoted, black balled or relegated to the D-list. Under such pressure and stress by sponsors, life becomes a merry-go-round of bouts with insanity and phoniness.

Michael Jordan net worth $1 billion:

Tyler Perry net worth $400 million.

Sean Combs net worth $750 million.

Bill Cosby net worth $350 million.

Dr. Dre net worth $710 million.

Shaquille O'Neal net worth $350 million.

* Tiger Woods is worth $700 million (some estimates say just $550 million).

Russell Simmons net worth $325 million.

Jay Z net worth $520 million.

Quincy Jones net worth $310 million.

Beyoncé net worth $300 million.

Floyd Mayweather net worth $280 million.

LeBron James net worth $270 million.

50 Cent net worth $270 million.

Kobe Bryant is worth $260 million.

Will Smith net worth $250 million.

*Derek Jeter net worth $185 million.

Serena Williams net worth $150 million.

Samuel L. Jackson net worth $150 million.

Denzel Washington net worth $150 million.

R. Kelly net worth $150 million.

Lil Wayne net worth $135 million.

Ice Cube net worth $120 million.

Snoop Dogg net worth $120 million.

Rihanna net worth $120 million.

Martin Lawrence net worth $110 million.

Usher net worth $110 million.

LL Cool J net worth $100 million.

Morgan Freeman net worth $90 million.

David Robinson net worth $90 million.

Kanye West net worth $90 million.

Tyra Banks net worth $90 million.

Jamie Foxx net worth $85 million.

*Pharrell Williams net worth $80 million.

Eddie Murphy net worth $75 million.

Venus Williams net worth $75 million.

Rev. Run net worth $70 million.

Halle Berry net worth $70 million.

Chris Rock net worth $70 million.

Sidney Poitier net worth $65 million.

Rapper T.I net worth $50 million.

Alicia Keys net worth $50 million.

*Kimora Lee Simmons net worth $50 million.

John Singleton net worth $50 million.

*Naomi Campbell net worth $48 million.

David Ortiz net worth $45 million.

Andre 3000 net worth $45 million.

Nicki Minaj net worth $45 million.

*Dennis Haysbert net worth $42 million.

Eriq La Salle net worth $40 million.

Spike Lee net worth $40 million.

Shonda Rhimes net worth $40 million.

Don Cheadle net worth $35 million.

Kandi Burruss net worth $35 million.

Kendrick Lamar net worth $33 million

Ice T net worth $30 million.

Terrence Howard net worth $30 million.

Kevin Hart net worth $25 million.

Angela Bassett net worth $20 million.

Jada Pinkett Smith net worth $20 million.

Antoine Fuqua net worth $18 million.

Nas 'Nasir Jones net worth $17 million.

Ving Rhames net worth $16 million.

Idris Elba net worth $15 million.

Forest Whitaker net worth $15 million.

Danny Glover net worth $15 million.

LeVar Burton net worth $14 million.

Nia Long net worth $13 million.

NeNe Leakes net worth $12 million

Gabrielle Union net worth $12 million.

Laila Ali net worth $10 million.

*Djimon Hounsou net worth $10 million.

*Zoe Saldana net worth $8 million.

Regina King net worth $10 million.

Taraji P. Henson net worth $6 million.

Billy Dee Williams net worth $7.5 million.

*Yo Gotti Net Worth $2.5million

Kerry Washington net worth $8 million.

Leverage

Too much **leverage** can be bad, but there's no hard and fast rule as to how much is too much. No matter what its use, [money] **leverage** can be a powerful tool when used responsibly.

Seminar Slide Samples & Guidance Points

Slide 1

Explain how and why the greatest resource of a community are developed God given talents in every person.

Community Row Homes   Single Homes

Mixed-Use Developement   Community Map Plan

What is a mix-use development?

Slide 2

Explain how and why gentrification affects low income communities.

Before   &   After

Is gentrification a benefit for communities?

Slide 3

Read each code and explain how southern black codes was the death of early communities.

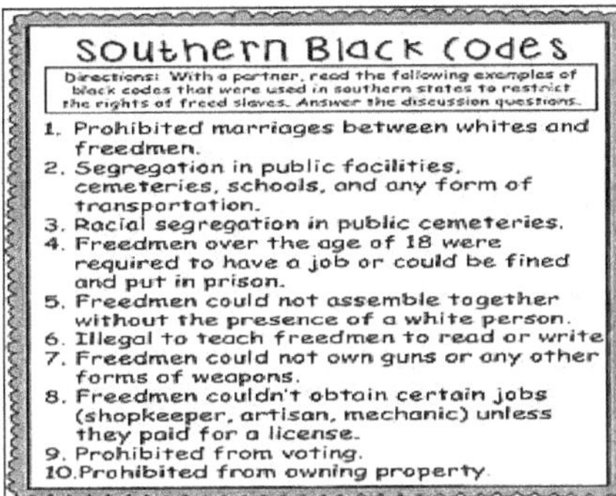

Was southern black codes a form of gentrification after 1877?

Slide 4

Explain how and why the greatest resource of Black Wall Street (Greenwood) of 1921 was the talents people used to build it.

Why was Greenwood burned to the ground by local government?

Before   &   After

<u>*Slide 5*</u>

Explain how and why the idea of expressways destroyed inner-cites where black communities were developing during the 1950's and early 60's.

Is building communities a form of warfare?

<u>*Slide 6*</u>

Explain how and why black communities suffer from high crime rates?

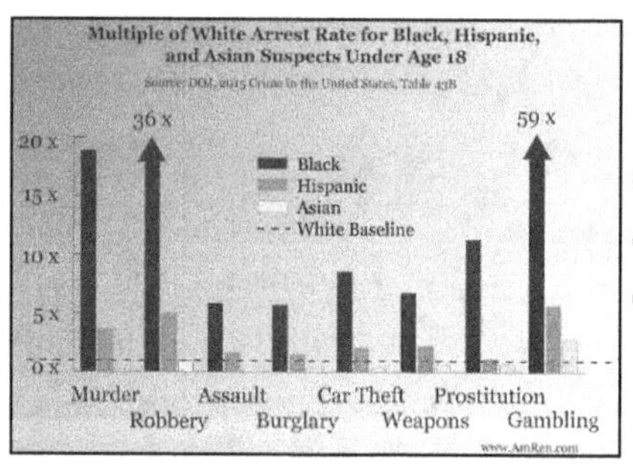

Can black communities reduce crime rates?

<u>*Slide 7*</u>

Explain why Muhammad's Economic Blueprint begins with Mosque, Training, University of Islam and Education

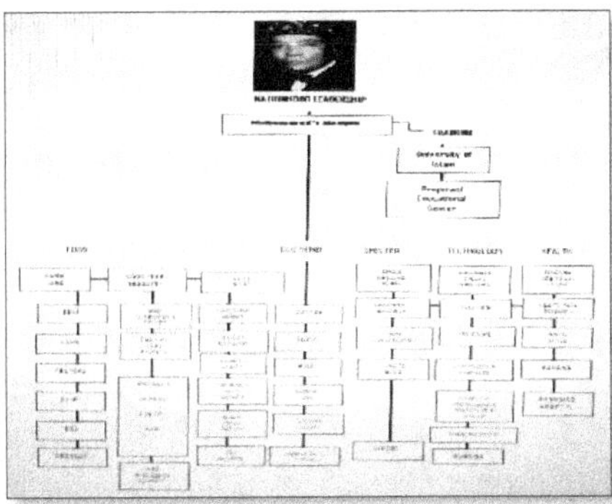

What is the cost of building a community?

<u>*Slide 8*</u>

Explain how to leverage high-net worth black entertainers to inspire black community to build towns again.

What does 18 billion dollar[s] net worth of 100 black celebrities mean compared to a town such as China Town in New York?

Slide 9

Nation: a large body of people united by common descent, history, culture, or language, inhabiting a particular country or territory.

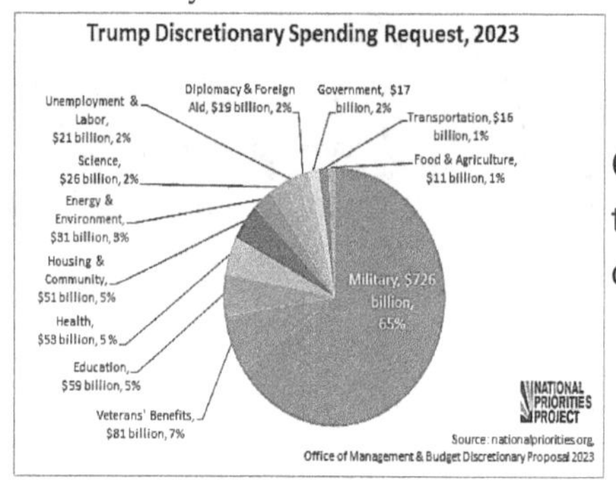

Can Black people fund their own communities?

Slide 10

Explain how the U.S. Government is funded.

Can Blacks of Northern Hemisphere be considered a nation, why?

<u>*Slide 11*</u>

Explain why black people migrated out of southern states and why they are moving back to southern states.

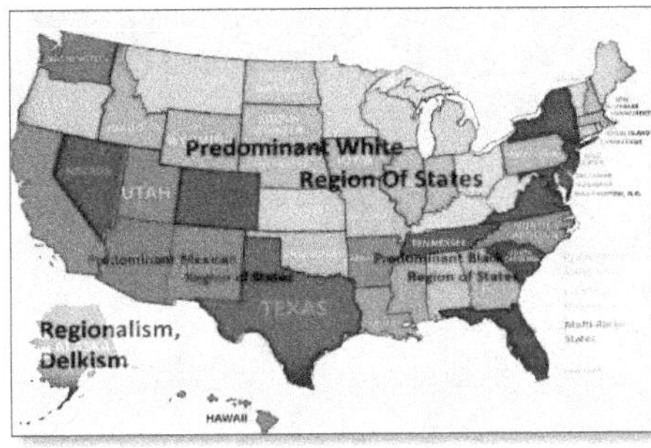

How can we begin building strong communities in southern states?

<u>*Slide 12*</u>

Explain why and how modern farming is the engine of a nation and our community.

How are *"friendships in all walks of life"* leveraged for political bonds in community building plans and completion?

- -

Now that you have read this book, to get involved with promoting our seminar, contact us by email: Benefitsofbuilding@gmail.com

www.ingramcontent.com/pod-product-compliance
Lightning Source LLC
Chambersburg PA
CBHW061511250726
48657CB00005B/1788